SOMERSET HOUSE W

Somerset House: The Indexes

Since January 1858, all wills have been proved in civil courts – either the Principal Probate Registry in London, or the offices of the District Probate Registries in various parts of the country. Wherever they were proved in England or Wales, the indexes have been combined centrally, and can be seen freely at Somerset House in The Strand, London. These annual indexes were printed, and sets are available at provincial centres, see back cover.

The Principal Probate Registry (now called The Principal Registry of the Family Division) in The Strand is at the back of the hollow square of buildings which form Somerset House and access is through the gateway from the Strand and across the car park (not intended for public use). Anyone can go there, between the hours of 10 a.m. and 4.30 p.m., from Mondays to Fridays, and look at the indexes of wills for nothing and actually see copies of the wills themselves, from all over England and Wales, for a small fee.

The *indexes* have the names of testators, filed in alphabetical order, according to the date when the will was proved, which may be a while after the person died. For every year from 1858 until about nine months from the current date, these indexes are all available in bound sets, with all the names in their alphabetical order. *Letters of Administration* (abbreviation: Admons.) might be issued if a person left no will *(Intestacy,* see below). These administrations are indexed in the same books, before 1870 following the wills, since then mixed in with them, always clearly indicated in the books themselves. The latest indexes are available in a computerised index, which is by no means simple to use.

The index entry in itself contains a great deal of valuable information. For a will, this may include the name of the deceased; possibly his occupation; his address when the will was made and any other address where a later codicil was made; the precise date and place of death; very occasionally the cause of death (*e.g.* a street accident); the date and court of the probate; the name(s) of the executor(s), the address, either occupation or relationship to the deceased, if stated in the will; if there are or were other executors named in the will; the amount of the estate sworn; and revisions of the figure made later; the date of any later grant (*e.g.* if an executor dies before completing his work.)

An Administration where there is a will but, for various reasons, no executor, shows the same details. An administration for a person who has made no will (see *Intestacy*) has the name and address of the deceased, the date of death, the date and place of the grant and the name of the administrator, who is normally the next of kin.

Seeing the Will

Where there is a will, it is almost always worth having a look at it. The exception is where the executor (or administrator) is described as *'universal legatee'*, since all the will says is *'all I possess to my dear wife Maggie'*. Otherwise when you have found the entry in the index, take the whole book to the counter on the left, where you will be asked if you want to see the will. Resist the temptation to be facetious – the alternative is to order a photo-copy, sight unseen, which is what the lads from the lawyers' offices do. It costs more, it is slower, but the client pays, so who cares.

The official will write the name and reference on a ticket – if there are two entries of the same name in the same year, make sure you point to the correct one upside-down. Then take the ticket along the corridor on the right to the Cashier's Office and pay 25p. Take the ticket back to the counter, and the official will hand it over to the porters.

While you take the index book back to its shelf – not forgetting to copy out the details first – the will copy or register is being found in the miles of shelving in the store. A London (Principal Probate Registry) will is located within ten minutes or less, but a 'country will' is stored further away and may take up to half an hour to be produced on a busy day. Each time the lift in the corner whines up, listen to the porters, who call out, not *your* name, but the name on the will. Signal when you hear it, and they put the will on a table for you to read, either opening the book or marking the place with a tag. These books are dirty, so don't go dressed in your best.

You can then read the will, or make an abstract from it, but not copy it down word for word. This senseless restriction doesn't matter, for once, because wills are full of legal gobbledegook and repetitions, which can be reduced considerably in volume. Make an abstract of the important bits, which are basically the names, addresses, relationships, details of legacies and any personal comments or special phrases which will illuminate the family history.

The older wills were copied in a large round handwriting, with occasional fancy twiddles, but with a bit of concentration, these can be mastered. The copy has to be exact, so if the testator wrote it himself, you may get the full flavour of Grandpa's mis-spellings and odd phraseology. If you doubt your ability or are running out of time, or just fancy the will for display, you can get a copy of the whole part of it after all, for about 25p a page. Since some wills run to a dozen pages, making an abstract is cheaper and much quicker, and not nearly as difficult as it seems. A tremendous lot of the verbiage will be standard phrases, which you can discard and the rest can be translated into a short form (see below).

What is a Will?.

A will makes provision for the disposal of real and personal estate belonging to the *Testator* or *Testatrix*. Real estate is free-hold houses, land (and peerage titles, where this applies). Personal estate is leasehold houses and land, stocks and shares, insurances, household goods, stock in trade, tools and implements, cash, debts owing, jewellery *etc.*, *etc*. All these possessions are to be shared out, usually among family and friends, in amounts of percentages laid down by the testator. This task is performed by the *Executor*, Executrix or executors appointed in the will, after he or she or they have obtained the right to do so by proving the will in the Probate Court.

Legacies – the money or property left by the testator – may dispose of property *absolutely* with no strings attached, or *conditionally*, with certain limitations. The most common limitation is a *life interest* or *life rent*, whereby the legatee (a widow or son, say) has the use of or income from the particular property for life, after which it passes to another named person. The person with the life interest cannot sell or otherwise dispose of the property and it is normally in the control of trustees (probably the same as the executors). A widow might lose her life interest in her husband's estate if she remarried or have the legacy greatly reduced. A legacy to a daughter might be withheld if she married without consent,or *'during couverture'* (while married) or while a particular husband lived. This was influenced by the law concerning married women's property (see below).

A will normally disposes of real estate first, then leaseholds, then business premises and equipment, then personal effects, then money. On the whole, provision was first made for the widow, who might be left the family home, or a smaller house, or an annuity bought from the estate or payable out of income from rents or a business, plus household furniture and effects. She might have these for life or until she remarried. Only legacies left *'absolutely'* or *'at her own dispose'* really belonged to her properly.

The children were dealt with next. The eldest son would expect to inherit most of the real estate and the family business, while his brothers would get subsidiary property or money to set them up in life. If, for any reason, the testator mistrusted the abilities of a particular son, he might leave him a life interest only, with remainder to a named brother or grandson, but he could not tie the hands of his heirs in perpetuity, only those then alive. Daughters were generally given a dowry when they married. Unmarried girls were expected to stay with Mother, though if they were 'on the shelf' already, Father might make generous provision for their old age, since no jobs would be open to them. Sons may be listed before daughters in a will, but if a mixed list is given, it is likely to be in order of age.

Bequests to remoter relatives and friends come next and these are often useful in adding to the family tree. Wills of spinsters and widows are particularly full of cousins and side branches of the family. It is never a waste of time to note down the details of these minor bequests, for, at the very least, they give an idea of the style and standard of living and the personal interests of the testator.

The will ends with a standard attestation clause to show that thetestator has formally adopted the document at his will and signed it in the presence of two witnesses. A blind or illiterate person can make a legal will, which is then read over to him before witnesses, and signed for him. If he puts his finger on the will (on the seal if any) and accepts it, it is legal. The witness should not be a beneficiary or the spouse of one. If such a person signs, the will is legal but the legacy is forfeit. From this section of the will, you will need only the date and signature, and any unusual circumstances, as above. The witnesses' names should be noted.

It is normal to include a clause leaving the residue of the estate to named persons. Even when the testator knows what he has to leave, this is advisable, since he could acquire more property or a legacy might lapse (see below). If the appointed executor cannot or will not act, the residuary legatee most closely related to the executor is made the administrator.

If the testator changes his mind after making the will, he can write a new one. Then he must destroy the old one, not just scribble on it, and say in the new one that he revokes all past wills. If he wants to keep most of the will but to revoke one legacy – to an erring son – or to add a bequest to a new infant, he can add a *codicil* dealing with this, which is proved with the original will. Care has to be taken that it does not contradict the will nor leave the same property twice, so it often takes a great many words to say what it means. The codicil must be signed and witnessed and attested like the will itself.

An executor or executors should be appointed by the testator to carry out the provisions of the will. His/their first duty is to arrange the funeral and provide for any emergency measures which must be taken in connection with the family or business of the deceased. He must then prepare a list of the property of the deceased with its value – on which the estate duty is levied – and take or have a solicitor take the will to probate. Of recent years, it has become a custom to appoint a firm of solicitors or bank as executor, or joint executor, but formally it was more usual for a relative to act – a widow or adult son – or a trusted business associate.

Once probate has been granted, the executor takes possession of the estate (from the Probate Judge, who has technically owned it since the death of the testator). He pays the debts – and gets in what is owing – hands over specific legacies, and sells whatever he has been instructed to sell, and transfers any property bequeathed to the legatee. The remaining estate is then distributed in sums or shares as ordered and the final account is made. This is the end of the task, if all the legacies are given absolutely.

If certain legacies were conditional, the executor's task may continue for years, and he will normally be appointed as *trustee*, since he is 'on trust' to fulfil the rest of the will. If money is to be invested and the income paid to named persons, then there are strict rules about the type of stock in which investments may be made. Trustees are normally impowered to take their expenses from the estate, and absolved from any losses caused accidentally or otherwise than by malpractice. If a trustee dies, others may be appointed. All this is detailed at great length and all you need to note is 'standard trustee clauses'.

Administration plus Will; Limitations; Scotland

Executors can refuse to take on the burden, or, having taken it on, they may resign or die before getting very far with the tasks involved. In that case, or where the testator fails to name an executor at all, an administrator is appointed by the court. This will normally be the residuary legatee who is next of kin to the deceased and able to act. If there is no residuary legatee, then the ordinary next of kin is appointed, or the principal legatee under the will. If the next of kin or residuary legatee is a minor, then the guardian can act. An administrator may be appointed if the executor named is abroad, goes mad, cannot cope with a legal dispute *etc*. In all these cases, there will be a will. For administration without a will, see *Intestacy*.

Wills are automatically revoked by marriage or remarriage, in England and Wales, unless they were made just before the wedding and '*in contemplation of marriage*', like the older marriage settlements. In Scotland, marriage does not revoke a will, but the birth of a child to the testator does. In England, the birth does not revoke a will and the father must make a codicil to include it, unless his will refers to '*all my children*' already. Scottish wills need not be signed by the testator in the presence of his witnesses, provided he tells them it is his will.

English law allows a person to dispose of his whole estate at whim, provided he is adult, sane, solvent and male. There were limitations on married women born and married before 1883 (see *Married Women's Property*). Idiots, persons of unsound mind at the time of making the will, persons suffering from brain damage *etc.*, cannot make a legal will, neither can minors (under 21 until the age of majority became 18), except for minor members of the armed forces in war or mariners in peril.

Bankrupts or persons heavily in debt cannot will away property to which their creditors are entitled, and debts will be a first charge on the estate, before any share-out is made. In fact, the heir of a bankrupt will at least be morally obliged to make good any deficit, especially if pre-death gifts were made to him after the testator's estate got rocky.

In Scotland, a married man with children may not dispose freely of his own estate. One third must go to the widow, one third to the children and only the last third – 'the deid's part' – may be left at whim. If there is a widow but no children, or children alone, then the reserved part is a half and the dead's part the other half. Minors may make legal wills in Scotland, though formerly only to dispose of personal estate. Scottish wills proved centrally or locally may be seen at the General Register House, Princes Street, Edinburgh.

Lapsed Legacies
The fact that a person was left something in a will does not prove that he got it. If a specific item – a house, a painting – was bequeathed, but sold before the testator died, the legacy lapsed. So did it if the legatee died before the testator, unless they died at the same time exactly, and then the older is deemed to have died first. If the legatee was child of the testator, by a legal fiction he or she was deemed to have died afterwards, even if the fact was that he/she died some years before. This meant that, if the son or daughter left children, they would inherit the legacy which would have come to their parent, sharing it (*per stirpes*).

Legacies are normally paid to minors only when they become 21 or marry and a testator can set 25 or later as the age for payment if he fancies doing so. If the legatee dies before reaching this age, then the legacy lapses, but it was usual to allow for this by leaving the *Remainder* to the child or children of the deceased legatee. Where a legacy was left to a group of people, as for instance, the children of a particular brother or sister, one or more of whom might die before getting their share, it could be arranged that the lapsed share went to all the others in the group in equal parts. The process was known as *benefit of survivorship* and several lines of the will explaining this can be reduced to '*ben.surv.*'

Married Women's Property
Until 1883, the ordinary married women had no property of her own, even the clothes she stood up in. '*Husband and wife are one person, and that person is the husband*' was the legal position. A wife could therefore not make a will. In certain circumstances, a father or other relative might leave a specific sum to the wife, with instructions that she should be allowed to dispose of it at death by 'a writing or deed' and these deeds of gift are proved like wills, but the system relied heavily on the cooperation of the husband, who could spend the money first. From 1883 onwards married women were allowed to dispose of money they owned at marriage or acquired in their own right after that date, but this did not apply retrospectively to women married before 1883, and they could only deal with what they acquired after that date, not the dowry they had on marriage, unless a super-indulgent husband allowed them to do so.

Cautious fathers and uncles, before and for some time after 1883, continued to leave property intended for married daughters to trustees, who were instructed to pay the income only to the wife, and sometimes specifying *'free from any debts or incumbrances of her present or any other husband'* and allowing her to have the principal only when widowed, or not at all, and giving the *'remainder'* to her children when of age.

This type of clause does not necessarily indicate that Father disliked the son-in-law, only the system, but if the trustees are instructed to pay the money *'as and when convenient'* and the husband is *'not to intermeddle'* with the arrangements, this may mean that Father suspects The Worst.

Warning

The existence of a legacy is no proof that it was paid to the person named, even if he/she survived the testator, and to the age laid down in a condition. Always add up the legacies and see if the total matches the estate. A man might dispose of property or lose his money after making his will and before dying. The executor had to pay for the funeral, the probate charges and then the debts. If the remaining estate was insufficient, real estate had to be sold to pay this and meet demands of the creditors. Only then would specific legacies be paid, and the residue, if any, divided. If the estate was not sufficient to meet all legacies, then they would, by agreement, be settled *pro rata*. There might be no residue left to share after that, to the loss of close family members.

Intestacy

If a man died without making a will, his estate was divided between his relatives according to certain rules, which have varied over the years. You can check the exact position most easily in an edition of *Whitaker's Almanack* for the appropriate year, which gives a simple summing up in comprehensible terms. Distribution depends on the number and closeness of surviving relatives.

Before 1926, real estate was treated separately from personal estate. If a man left a widow and children, the widow got a life interest in a third of the real estate and the eldest son the rest. If there were children only, the eldest son took the lot. If he had died before, leaving heirs, his son (or sons in succession) inherited. If he left daughters, they shared equally. If the line of the eldest son failed, then the next brother and his heirs inherited, and so on. A childless wife got her third and the husband's father, or his brothers in turn, their heirs, sisters sharing, grandparents, uncles and aunts and their heirs could take the rest, in sequence as above, with closer relatives always preferred to distant ones, and males of any group to females. If there were no relatives, the widow got her third for life and the crown took the rest.

Personal estate, which included leaseholds, together with real estate after 1926, was placed in the hands of an administrator and turned into money, which was then disributed to relatives with a claim. A husband took the lot until recently and a widow would get the whole of a 'small estate' only. 'Small' was set at different levels at different dates. In 1890, the amount was £500, in 1926 it was £1,000 and 'personal chattels'; of recent years, the 'small estate' increased to £15,000 and personal effects. Everything above that amount was shared according to the amount and relationship of family left by the deceased.

In 1890, the widow got a third, the children two-thirds. From 1926, the widow got a life interest in half the residue, the children the rest. Nowadays, the childless widow gets £40,000 before division. In 1890, if there were no other relatives than the widow, the Crown took half the estate, now the widow gets it all, just as a man would have done anyway. If there are no blood relatives within the prescribed degrees (that is, sharing common grandparents) the State takes all.

Large sums advanced to relatives by the deceased and (before 1926) real estate inherited through him, had to be 'put into hotchpot' or included in the gross value of the estate and as part of that person's share. An illegitimate child had no automatic right of inheritance at all, and could not claim anything from his father, only from his mother. Nowadays an illegitimate child has a right of inheritance, but obviously has to prove paternity or show it was admitted in the father's lifetime.

Lapsed legacies which had not been remaindered, and the share of a residuary legatee who died first, if there was no benefit of survivorship clause, were treated as part of the estate, and distributed according to the laws of intestacy.

Administrators would be appointed by the Probate Court, and would normally be the next of kin, unless that person was a minor, absent from England *etc.*, a bankrupt, or incapable mentally. In the case of a minor, the natural guardian was made administrator (a grandfather or uncle, say) and the minor could take over and administer when he came of age, if all the assets had not then been distributed. If the testator was insolvent, the major creditor/s might be appointed to wind up the estate, or a Probate Court official.

Despite the Englishman's general power to dispose of his estate at whim, cutting out his nearest and supposedly dearest, dependent persons could always claim maintenance from an estate of sufficient size. Dependants were widows; minor children; unmarried daughters of any age; sons of full age disabled mentally or physically; orphan grandchildren. More recently, illegitimate children and 'common law' wives have been able to claim, if they could prove they were normally supported by the deceased. This is a difficult matter if the man covers his tracks well or used a fictitious name. Ladies with children of assorted parentage were unlikely to succeed.

Making an Abstract of a Will

Wills of the nineteenth century were written without internal punctuation except full stops, which makes them look daunting. But they can be broken up into comprehensible chunks and reduced vastly in size:

'*...I give and bequeath to my dearly beloved wife Martha Jane Toogood all that my freehold messuage and tenement known by the name of the Limes Acacia Avenue Southern Road in the parish of Croynge in the county of Surrey with all appurtenances thereunto belonging and I also give and bequeath to the aforesaid Martha Jane Toogood all that paddock adjoining unto the aforesaid messuage and tenement containing half an acre of land and also to the aforesaid Martha Jane Toogood all those my four freehold cottages situated at and formerly known by the name of Nos 37 to 50 Gasworks Alley and now or lately known as Nos 50 to 56 Dawkins Road in the parish of Stockham in the aforesaid county all of which premises aforesaid to remain to the aforesaid Martha Jane Toogood during her natural life provided always that she remain my widow and from the date of her decease or intermarriage with any other husband I give and bequeath the aforesaid messuage and tenement known as the Limes Acacia Avenue Croynge and also the afore mentioned appurtenances thereunto and also the paddock adjoining the aforesaid premises containing half an acre and all those freehold cottages known formerly as Nos. 47 to 50 Gasworks Alley and now or late as Nos. 50 to 56 Dawkins Road Stockham aforesaid to my eldest son Josiah Mutch Toogood to have and to hold for him and his heirs forever provided that he pays out of the proceeds of the*

*aforesaid messuage or tenement, paddock and four freehold cottages theretofore
above more exactly described the undermentioned sums of money to his sisters
hereinafter named that is to say to my daughter Mary Ann Martha Toogood the sum
of one hundred and fifty pounds and to my daughter Eliza Jane Spratt the wife of
John Spratt ironmonger and oil and colourman of Poynders Lane in the parish of
Croynge aforesaid the sum of fifty pounds and to my daughter Sarah Ann Gubbins
widow late the wife of George Gubbins horticultural sundriesman of Stockham
High Road the sum of fifty pounds likewise within six months of the day when he
shall take possession of the premises aforesaid after the decease or intermarriage of
his aforesaid mother Martha Jane Toogood whichever shall happen first provided
always that if the aforesaid Mary Ann Martha Toogood shall happen to die before
the decease or intermarriage of my aforesaid wife Martha Jane Toogood then the
sum of one hundred and fifty pounds heretofore given to the aforesaid Mary Ann
Martha shall remain to her lawful child or children if she die possessed of any such
to any son or sons that attain the age of twenty one years or to any daughter or
daughters that shall attain the age of twenty one years or shall marry before that age
with the consent and approbation of my son Josiah Mutch Toogood their uncle in
equal portions share and share alike but failing such issue lawful that the aforesaid
sum shall remain and be given to my aforesaid son Josiah Mutch Toogood and to
my daughter Eliza Jane Spratt and to my daughter Sarah Ann Gubbins and to my
son Henry Knott Toogood in equal shares to such of them as shall be living. And as
to the sum of fifty pounds above bequeathed to my daughter Eliza Jane Spratt if she
should happen to die before the said legacy become due and payable then I give and
bequeath the aforesaid fifty pounds to the child or children of the aforesaid Eliza
Jane Spratt then living at the date when the aforesaid Josiah Mutch Toogood shall
take possession of the said premises to any child or children being a son at the age of
twenty one and to any child or children being daughters at the age of twenty one or
shall marry first with the consent and approbation of my son Josiah Mutch
Toogood their uncle in equal shares. And as to the fifty pounds above bequeathed to
my daughter Sarah Ann Gubbins widow aforesaid if she should happen to die before
the said legacy shall become due and payable then I give and bequeath the said fifty
pounds to my aforesaid son Josiah Mutch Toogood and my daughter Eliza Jane
Spratt or the survivor of them in equal shares. To Elizabeth Jane Toogood the wife
of my son Henry Knott Toogood I bequeath the sum of six shillings per week to be
paid into her own hand by my son Josiah Mutch Toogood at his discretion and the
aforesaid sum is not to be charged with any debt or incumbrance of her aforesaid
husband my son Henry Knott Toogood for her lifetime while she remain my son's
wife or widow and not after that and if she happen to die or being a widow to
remarry with any other man then the aforesaid sum of six shillings per week to be
laid out by my aforesaid son Josiah Mutch Toogood for the maintenance and
benefit of Henry Wilbe Toogood my grandson until he attains the age of twenty one.
To my aforesaid grandson Henry Wilbe Toogood the sum of one hundred and fifty
pounds when he shall attain the age of twenty one years and I earnestly entreat him
that he shall at all times take the counsel and advice of his uncle Josiah Mutch
Toogood as to his advancement in life...'*

This can be reduced to:-

*'To d.b. wife MARTHA JANE TOOGOOD, my residence, The Limes, Acacia
Ave., Croynge, Sy, plus paddock ½ acre adj. plus 4 freehold cottages ex 47-50
Gasworks Alley now 50-56 Dawkins Road, Stockham, Sy, for life while widow.*

Rem. on death or marriage to eldest son JOSIAH MUTCH TOOGOOD on condn. he pays to his sisters as foll:-
    to my dau MARY ANN MARTHA TOOGOOD, £150
    to my dau ELIZA JANE SPRATT wife of JOHN S. ironmonger + oil & colourman, Poynders Lane, Croynge, £50
    to my dau SARAH ANN GUBBINS wid of GEORGE G. hortic. sundriesman of Stockham High Rd, £50
    If MAMT dies pre payt, then to legit issue sons 21, daus 21 or marr with consent of JMT or if d.s.l.p. rem. to JMT, EJS, SAG and my son HENRY KNOTT TOOGOOD, = shares ben. surv.
    If EJS dies pre payt, then to living issue, sons 21 daus 21 or marr consent JMT
    If SAG dies pre payt, rem. to JMT, EJS, = shares ben. surv.
    To ELIZABETH JANE wife of my son HKT 6 sh per week, paid to her by JMT "not chargeable with debts of HKT" for life while marr to HKT or his widow. If d or re-mar then 6sh per wk to her son HENRY WILBE TOOGOOD for maint & ben while under 21. At 21 HWT to have £150, "earnestly entreat him at all times to take counsel and advice of uncle JMT as to his advancement in life".'

Write all names in full for the first time, then the initials, unless two legatees have the same. Include the surnames of daughters, to show which are married at the time of making the will. Indicate relationships clearly: 'my dau', 'his dau', not just 'dau'. Note the type, amount and limitations of legacies and what happens if it lapses. List all addresses – to help census and other searches – including those of people apparently unrelated, who may turn turn out to be aunties. Copy lists of items specifically bequeathed – individual pieces of furniture, portraits *etc.*, may still be around, and a good list will give you an idea of the standard of living at least. Copy verbatim any odd remarks and phrases which do not immediately make sense, or comments which throw light on family relationships.

Note the names of executor/s and residuary legatees and the date of will and codicils if any.

Useful abbreviations

If 'X' d.s.p. (or *d.s.l.p.*) = if 'X' dies without issue, or without legitimate issue.
21 or marr. = at the age of 21 or marriage before that.
rem. = remainder, what happens to the legacy when someone dies or another limitation happens.
= *shares* : in equal shares, share and share alike.
ben.surv. = benefit of survivorship, so if one of a group of named persons dies, the rest get it.
exor., exex. = executor, executrix.
resid. = all the residue of an estate not otherwise bequeathed in detail.
trustee/s = person/s appointed *on trust* to carry out certain provisions, often long term in action. Trustees are governed by strict laws and may not invest in speculative schemes ('approved stocks' may be mentioned) or benefit from the trust monies.
per stirpes = by descent. A share which would have gone to a deceased parent is shared by all the children equally, however many there are.
hotchpot = the total value of the estate which is to be divided between heirs. Advances already made can be treated as part of this.

It isn't there !

A will is not necessarily proved in the year the person died, so look onwards – it may take years to settle an estate. In the last century, if a widow and young children were left, there may have been no need to go to probate till the children were adult. An older widow with adult children comfortably established might succeed without formality and probate would come when she died, possibly twenty years later. Small estates could be passed on without attracting estate duty, so wills may not have been made or proved formally.

There may be no will for a person who was affluent in life. He – especially she – may have been enjoying life interests and annuities, which left no disposable estate. Look for the wills of the older generation of the family to establish this. Before 1890, some family estates were controlled by marriage settlements and later by family trusts, which operated like a life interest.

Postal Applications

You can write to the Correspondence Division, Principal Registry of the Family Division, Somerset House, Strand, London WC2R 1LP, and ask them to search for a will, if you know the date of death, within a year or so. For a fee of £2 they will search three years for the probate entry and tell you how much a photostat will cost at 25p a page. They don't make abstracts and it may take a fortnight or so for a reply. If the will doesn't turn up in three years, you will have to pay another fee for the next. All prices subject to review and increase.

District Probate Registries and Indexes

There are thirty District Probate Registries distributed throughout England and Wales, in which persons resident in that area could prove wills, although they could also use the Principal Registry in London. Until 1929, each local Registry was issued with a set of indexes for the whole of England and Wales each year, though copies of the actual wills were held in London and the registry where they were proved only. Recently, most District Registries have handed over these indexes and often their own locally proved wills before 1929 to the nearest County Record Office or other approved repository.

It is possible to obtain photostat copies of locally proved wills after 1929 from the District Registries, if details of name, date and place of death are sent, for a fee of 25p per page. For earlier wills, or where the place of probate is uncertain, it is best to send to London as above. Personal searchers should be able to obtain copies of wills in the District Registries, but protracted general searches may be difficult. Not all the repositories to which pre 1929 wills have been transferred have facilities for photocopying large documents.

The location of present District Probate Registries and Sub-Registries is given below. For full address, see telephone directory. Unless shown otherwise, these no longer hold the annual printed indexes or calendars, 1858-1928, and, where known, the present location of these is given. In most cases, pre-1929 registered copy and original wills have also been transferred elsewhere. Details are given in *Probate Jurisdictions: Where to Look for Wills,* by J.S.W.Gibson, 3rd edition, F.F.H.S. 1989.

District Probate Registries and Indexes

Avon: Bristol (*indexes from 1901*).
  Indexes (1858-1900): Bristol Record Office.
Bedfordshire: *Indexes:* Bedfordshire Record Office.
Cambridgeshire: Peterborough.
  Indexes (to 1934): Cambridgeshire Record Office, Cambridge.
Cheshire: Chester. *Indexes:* Chester Record Office.
Cornwall: Bodmin (also *indexes*).
Cumbria: Carlisle.
  Indexes: Cumbria Record Office, Carlisle.
Devon: Exeter (also *indexes*).
Gloucestershire: Gloucester.
  Indexes: Gloucestershire Record Office (daily charge).
Greater Manchester: Manchester.
  Indexes: Greater Manchester County R.O. (notice required).
Hampshire: Winchester. *Indexes:* Hampshire Record Office.
Humberside: Hull.
Kent: Maidstone.
Lancashire: Lancaster.
  Indexes: Lancashire Record Office, Preston.
Leicestershire: Leicester (*indexes from 1887*).
  Indexes, 1858-1886: Leicestershire R.O. (notice required).
Lincolnshire: Lincoln. *Indexes (to 1933):* Lincolnshire Archives Office.
Merseyside: Liverpool. *Indexes:* Liverpool Record Office.
West Midlands: Birmingham.
  Indexes: Birmingham Reference Library (Archives Department).
Norfolk: Norwich.
  Indexes (to 1937): Norwich Local Studies Library.
Northamptonshire: *see* Cambridgeshire.
Northumberland: *see* Tyne and Wear.
Notts.: Nottingham. *Indexes:* Nottinghamshire Archives Office.
Oxfordshire: Oxford.
  Indexes: Bodleian Library (Radcliffe Camera) (daily charge).
Staffordshire: Stoke-on-Trent.
Suffolk: Ipswich (no indexes held locally).
East Sussex: Brighton.
  Indexes: East Sussex Record Office, Lewes.
Tyne and Wear: Newcastle-upon-Tyne (no indexes held locally).
North Yorkshire: Middlesbrough.
  York (also *Indexes*).
South Yorkshire: Sheffield.
  Indexes: Sheffield R.O., Sheffield Central Library (prior notice required; no public access, staff undertake short searches).
West Yorkshire: Leeds.
  Indexes: West Yorkshire County Record Office, Wakefield.
Clwyd: *Indexes:* Clwyd Record Office, Ruthin.
Dyfed: Carmarthen.
  Indexes: National Library of Wales, Aberystwyth (to 1972).
  Dyfed Archives, Carmarthen Branch Office.

Glamorgan: Llandaff.
  Indexes: Glamorgan Archive Service, Cardiff.
Gwynedd: Bangor.
  Indexes: Gwynedd Archives Service, Caernarfon Area R.O.